BLUE
DIESELS
IN VIEW

GAVIN MORRISON

Rails

Introduction

The 'Blue Diesel' era covered in this book began in June 1964, when British Railways steam still had another four years to go. The livery first appeared in the form of a demonstration train of new Mk1 coaches, released form Derby works and given the code XP64. A new Brush Type 4 locomotive was painted in a blue livery to match, with a half yellow cab end and a red panel on the side of the cab, plus the BR arrow logo. The shade of blue used was slightly lighter than the one which became the standard.

A period of around 20 years then followed of the blue era, regarded by many as one of the most uninteresting periods of all on our railways. This may have been true as far as photography was concerned, especially as the age of colour film was taking hold for many photographers. But looking back today, what the railway may have lacked in colour variety it certainly made up for in the variety of locomotive classes and train types and railway infrastructure, such as signals, the large gantries and signal boxes.

As is so often the case with many things the pendulum has swung to the other extreme, with vast numbers of different liveries of every colour, which are always changing. Glorified bus shelters have now replaced the station waiting rooms at many stations, especially in the north of the country. Many locations and fine railway structures have now gone from view as far as photographs are concerned due to dense undergrowth and trees, not to mention the palisade fencing. Whether one compensates the other is open to debate, but there are still thousands of photographers about recording the network.

With a book of this size one can only scratch the surface of what was on offer during the period. I have decided to split it into regions to try and give some coverage to the whole network. It is not intended to show every class that received the blue livery. In some cases the earlier small classes only had one or two examples that were painted in blue. A small selection of DMUs has been included and the plain blue livery on some of the classes must surely have been the dullest ever applied to rolling stock.

During this period there were relatively few new locomotive classes introduced. The arrival of the HSTs in the late 1970s was undoubtedly the most significant event.

The introduction of the large BR arrow on the side of many classes was a huge improvement to the appearance of them. By this very simple modification to the livery many classes looked very impressive.

With the incredible expansion of the preservation movement we are fortunate to still be able to see blue diesels from this period in action. A Class 47 in plain blue livery today creates much interest, especially on the main line. It was a little different when there were over 500 of them in use.

Gavin Morrison

Contents

Title page Class 40 No 40069 has just emerged from Standedge tunnel, built between 1890 and 1894 and three miles and 64 yards long. In addition to this bore there are two single bore tunnels, the older having been constructed between 1846 and 1849. There is also a canal tunnel under the north tunnel. The two single bore tunnels are not now in use; both pass under the Pennines between Marsden and Diggle. The north tunnel had water troughs inside it which were 560 and 563 yards long. The train is the 8.55 Saturdays only York–Llandudno. No 40069 entered service in April 1960 for WCML services and was withdrawn on 18th September 1983.

Cockwood Harbour has been a favourite photographic location for many years. Here Class 52 No D1035 'Western Yeoman' passes with a down express. I was fortunate on this occasion to get a photo with some water in the harbour as it fills and empties very quickly. D1035 was the first of the class to be built at Crewe works in June 1962, but like the rest of the class had a short career, which ended on 5th January 1975.

Scottish Region

The 50-mile branch of the Highland Railway from Dingwall was completed when Kyle of Lochalsh station opened on 2nd November 1897 and it is still open today. In steam days there was a small sub-shed to Inverness with a turntable and the turntable pit was still in existence when this picture was taken. Class 24 No 5121 is in the station ready to return to Inverness having worked in on a morning train. The Isle of Skye can be seen in the background. D5121 went new to Inverness depot in June 1960 and was renumbered 24121 in May 1974. It was withdrawn in December 1976. *Date 10th March 1973.*

The 10.30 departure from Inverness (The Clansman) is shown leaving past Welsh's Bridge on its 10 hour plus journey to Euston. In the latter part of its journey it will leave the WCML at Stafford and travel via Wolverhampton and Birmingham New Street. On this day Class 47/4 No 47562 'Sir William Burrell' is in charge. It was new as No D1617 in September 1964 and then carried the following numbers: 47036, 47562, 47672 and 47760. It was involved in a bad collision on 11th November 1993 at Leeds and it later caught fire on the 13th March 2001 whilst working the 00.55 Bristol–Penzance TPO at Rattery. It survived both these incidents and is now working in the West Coast Railways fleet. *Date 18th April 1986.*

Culloden viaduct is a few miles south of Inverness on the ex-Highland Railway. It crosses a wide valley through which the River Nairn passes. The viaduct is also known by the names Nairn and Clava. It has 29 spans with a total length of 600 yards, each span being 50 feet, with the middle one being 100 feet and 132 feet above the river. It was opened in 1898 with the direct route to Inverness from Aviemore. Not as well known as some other viaducts in the UK it is certainly one of the most impressive. It is a Category 'A' listed structure and the longest masonry one in Scotland. Seen at the south end are two Class 37/0, No 37113 and No 37160, heading an up freight. No 37113 was allocated to Tinsley depot at the time, while 37160 was Motherwell based. No 37113 was new as D6813 in February 1963 while 37160 as D6860 arrived the following July. The end of 37113 came when it ran away at Edinburgh Waverley on 13th August 1994 hitting HST power car No 43180. It was cut up at MC Metals in August 1995. No 37160 was withdrawn in December 1993. *Date 17th September 1987.*

Class 47/4 No 47586 with wrap-round yellow front ends is seen leaving the south end of Perth station on a summer Saturdays only 08.30 Inverness–Bristol. Initially the station at Perth was used by many small companies, but takeovers reduced them to three by 1866 – Caledonian, North British and the Highland Railway. This photograph shows the ex-Highland Railway side of the station with the Caledonian part to the right. No 47586 entered service in October 1964 and carried numbers D1623/47042/47586 and 47676 before being authorised for component recovery on 22nd October 1994. It was eventually scrapped during April 1998. *Date 5th July 1986.*

The 09.25 Aberdeen–Birmingham New Street is seen passing Bonnybridge Junction where the line from Perth and the north meets the Edinburgh Waverley to Glasgow Queen Street route. The train is being hauled by Class 47/0 No 47211 which was allocated to Haymarket depot at the time. It carried different numbers starting with D1861 when new in August 1965, followed by 47211 then 47394 and back to 47211. It was sold to Fragonset Railways in September 2002. Cutting up started on the 28th May 2003. *Date 5th September 1980.*

Later on the same day as the previous picture on page 7, Class 47/0 No 47211 returned north for a down express. It would have worked south as far as Mossend and then been replaced by electric power. Here it is shown passing Whifflet near Motherwell. *Date 5th September 1980.*

Right The West Highland extension from at Fort William to Mallaig Junction is 41 miles long and was opened in 1901. Eastfield depot allocated Class 37/0 No 37178 is crossing Lochnan Uamh viaduct, also known as Gleann Mama viaduct, 26 miles from Fort William and at the start of the 1 in 48 gradient up Beasdale bank which is just under two miles long. The viaduct is of concrete construction, like the most famous structure on the line, Glenfinnan Viaduct. It has eight 50ft arches and it is recorded that Bonny Prince Charlie left here on 20th September 1746 for France after the failure of the Jacobite rebellion. No 37178 was new in October 1963 as D6878 until selected by EWS for component recovery in 2000, but it was not withdrawn until 2005. It was bought by Harry Needle Rail Ltd, overhauled and sold to Network Rail. It is still in service as No 97303. *Date 31st July 1984.*

Fort William shed closed to steam in 1962. As can be seen nothing was done to house the new diesels, which were left outside. Class 27 Sulzer diesels took over virtually all the West Highland workings, and on this day Nos 5360 [later 27014], 5414 [27043], 5401 [27056] and 5397 [27053] were present. Ben Nevis at 4411 feet above sea level can be seen in the background. *Date 5th June 1971.*

A special No 1Z27 run by Pathfinder Tours ran on 18th, 19th and 20th of September 1987 from Bristol to Mallaig and return. Named the 'Son of Skirl' this is seen on the Saturday morning pulling away from Bridge of Orchy en route to Fort William. The locomotives are Nos 37092 and 37043, both allocated to Eastfield depot in Glasgow at the time. No 37092 was new in February 1963 as D6792. It was never officially withdrawn but was scrapped in October 2001. No 37043 was new in June 1962, numbered D6743, and was scrapped at Sims, Beeston in May 2003. *Date 19th September 1987.*

Oban station was opened on 1st July 1880. It has the impressive backdrop of McCaigs Tower situated on the top of Battery Hill. It was constructed between 1897 and 1901 by wealthy businessman John Stewart McCaig to provide work for local stonemasons during the winter months. It is a monument to his family and was intended to become a museum and art gallery, which has never been achieved. In the station is Class 37/0 No 37081 ready to leave with the 13.00 departure to Glasgow Queen Street. It was one of the first batch of Class 37s allocated to the West Highland services in 1979 and was named 'Loch Long' in 1981. It has a small non-standard white band along the bottom of the body, a feature of some of the Eastfield allocated members of the class. It entered service in November 1962 as D6781 and was renumbered 37797 in 1986 and eventually scrapped in 2006. Just to the right of the picture is the original Callander and Oban Station, which was of wooden construction. It was demolished in April 1987. *Date 3rd May 1984.*

Class 37/0 No 37081 is seen again but this time at Taynuilt station, 13 miles from Oban. Another class 37/0, No 37175, is in the station en route to Oban to collect the fuel tanks from the harbour. No 37175 was new in September 1963 as D6875 and was withdrawn in June 1999. It was bought for preservation in 2004 and in due course sold to Colas Rail. It is currently part of the fleet working on the network. *Date 3rd May 1984.*

Class 47/4 No 47586 is seen with a hybrid version of the standard BR blue livery, small emblem on the bodysides, all over yellow ends, including the cab sides and doors, and with black window surrounds and roof. Here it is shown leaving Keith on the 10.25 from Inverness to Aberdeen, which is 54 miles to the east. Keith is in the heart of the Scotch whisky distillery business. No 47586 was new in October 1964 as D1623, then 47042, 47586 and finally 47676. It was withdrawn and broken up in April 1998. *Date 30th March 1987.*

Aberdeen station sees Class 25 No 25008 waiting on a van train ready to leave for the south. Taken in the days of semaphore signals at the station, No 25008 was one of the early members of the class entering service in July 1961 as D5158 at Thornaby depot. It spent most of its career in Scotland until an accident caused its withdrawal in June 1980. *Date 2nd September 1977.*

The superb signal gantries at the south end of Aberdeen station provided an excellent setting for trains leaving the station. This picture was taken from one of these gantries and shows the Skyline of the 'Granite City' to advantage. Class 40 No 40165 is heading an up express to Glasgow or Edinburgh. No 40165 was allocated new to Haymarket depot as D365 in November 1961, where it stayed for its entire career which ended in July 1981. *Date 2nd September 1977.*

There are two viaducts immediately to the south of Montrose station. The one shown here is the Rossie viaduct designed by Sir Thomas Bouch, consisting of 17 brick arches and is 275m long. It is also known as the Inchbraoche viaduct and is a listed structure as it is the only surviving Bouch designed structure left in current use. The other one nearer the station is the South Esk and is a 16 bowed iron lattice girder design. After the Tay bridge disaster the authorities considered it unwise to allow Bouch to design this one. Both carry only a single line out to Usan which has caused operating difficulties on the route to this day. An up express headed by Class 40 No 40168 is heading south. It was new as No D368 in December 1961 and was another member of the class that spent almost its entire career allocated to Haymarket depot. It was withdrawn in November 1984. *Date 18th April 1981.*

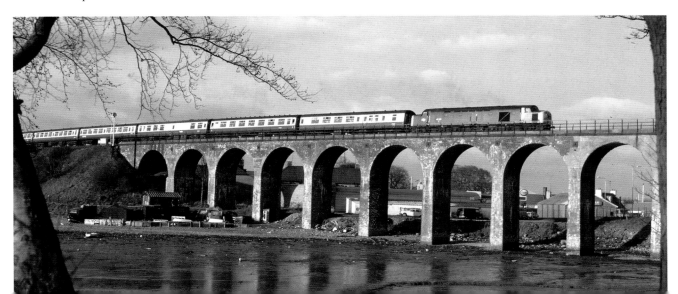

The Firth of Forth and the docks at Burntisland in Fife are clearly seen as Class 27/0 No 27025 leaves the station, on the 08.30 from Dundee to Edinburgh Waverley. No 27025 went to the North Eastern region at Thornaby when new in January 1962 numbered D5371. Its move to Scotland came in October 1969 where it remained until withdrawn in July 1987. *Date 5th July 1976.*

The days when the Class 06 Andrew Barclay diesel shunters were used in the Dundee Docks were over when this picture was taken. Nos 06006 and 06005 are dumped in the yard just outside Dundee station. Their original numbers when new in March and April 1959 were D2422 and D2423. Both were withdrawn in 1980. *Date 19th April 1981.*

Class 26 No 26026 is heading an up evening mixed train on the north to south side [main line] of the triangle just to the north of Inverkeithing station. The lines to the left go to Dunfermline and continue to complete the Fife circle. No 26026 was allocated to Scotland when new in May 1959, numbered D5326 and it remained north of the border until withdrawn in November 1992. *Date 10th August 1983.*

Scotland had an allocation of the Class 20s, mainly for working coal traffic in the coalfields of Fife and Ayrshire. No 20201 is seen with some empty MGR wagons, climbing the gradient from Inverkeithing past Jamestown to the Forth Bridge. No 20201 was new as D8301 to the North Eastern region and was allocated to Scotland in June 1976. It was withdrawn in September 1988. *Date 21st April 1981*

A Class 101 Metro-Cammell DMU is crossing the Forth Bridge as it approaches North Queensferry station with a morning commuter service from Edinburgh. The class was built between 1956 and 1960 and was the most numerous and successful of all the DMUs. There were 637 vehicles in the class of which 364 were powered. After 47 years service the last sets were withdrawn on the 21st December 2003.
Date 21st December 2003.

Cowlairs incline starts off the platform end at Glasgow Queen Street in a tunnel. It is about one and a half miles long with a gradient of 1 in 41. Built in 1842 it was originally rope worked by a steam engine at the top until 1848. It was then wire worked until 1908, although banking engines had also been used during this period. Afterwards all trains were banked until steam ended in the mid 1960s. Today the DMUs and soon to be electrics tackle it with relative ease. Class 47/4 No 47541 named 'The Queen Mother' at the time and allocated to Eastfield depot is descending the incline with the 14.35 from Aberdeen to Queen Street. No 47541 was new as D1755 in August 1964. It was allocated number 47161 (this was never applied), followed by 47541 and finally 47773. It is still regularly seen on the network and is based at Tyseley. *Date 2nd August 1983.*

This view of Eastfield depot at Glasgow is at the east end. It was by far the biggest diesel depot in the Scottish region. At this time there was a bridge across the depot which used to carry an ex-Caledonian line from the Maryhill area round to Balornock, from which this view could be photographed. *Date 4th September 1977.*

Locomotives which had visited St Rollox works for overhaul came to Eastfield for running in before returning to their home depots. The North British works at Cowlairs closed in 1968. Two immaculate class 27s, Nos 27005 and 27008, with class 26 No 26046 at the rear, have just arrived at the depot. These may well have been their last major overhauls as 27005 passed into preservation at the Bo'ness & Kinneil Railway in July 1987. *Date 30th April 1984.*

One of the Class 47s modified for push-pull working in Scotland and designated as a Class 47/7 is seen passing Eastfield depot hauling a Glasgow Queen Street evening service. The special DBSOs (Driving Brake Standard Open) were worked from the west end of the train. No 47706 was named 'Strathclyde'at the time and had entered service in March 1966 numbered D1936. It was renumbered 47494 in 1974 and converted to push/pull in 1979. Withdrawal came in April 1995 and it was broken up in August. *Date 30th April 1984.*

The Alva branch to the east of Stirling branched off at Cambus on the line to Alloa. It lost its passenger services in 1954 but at Menstrie, the station before Alva, there was a business processing molasses. The branch was kept open for this traffic as far as Menstrie. Class 26 No 26014 is shown on the branch returning with the tanks. No 26014 entered service in January 1959 numbered D5314. It was withdrawn in 1992. It was sold into preservation at the Caledonian Railway at Brechin, arriving in November 1994 after asbestos removal.
Date 14th June 1991.

This sort of freight has now vanished from the railways. Class 26 No 26013 in immaculate external condition potters along the Glasgow–Edinburgh main line at Gogar Bank just to the west of where Edinburgh Park Station now exists. No 26013 entered service in January 1959 numbered D5313. Initially it went to the Eastern Region but after three months moved to Scotland where it remained until withdrawn in March 1985, although it was not scrapped until 1987. *Date 21st April 1981.*

Over the years the east end of Haymarket diesel depot has produced some impressive line-ups of locomotives. On this day Deltic Class 55 No 55013 'The Black Watch' was alongside Class 40 No 40061 and Class 47/4 No 47555 'The Commonwealth Spirit'. At this period this locomotive was regularly used by the London Midland Region for Royal train duties. No 55013 was new to Haymarket in September 1961 where it remained until transferred to York in May 1979. It was withdrawn in December 1981. No 40061 also went new to Haymarket as D261 in February 1960 where it put in 13 years of service before moving to the London Midland Region from where it was withdrawn in June 1983. No 47555 was new from the Brush works in February 1964 numbered D1717. It became No 47126 in 1974 and 47555 in September 1974. It was stored in 1992 but was reinstated for special duties until withdrawal in 1999. *Date 21st April 1981.*

Until the electrification of the lines, Princess Street Gardens Edinburgh was a favourite location for enthusiasts to watch and photograph the trains. Local and express services to the north and west as well as freight all passed. Here we see three of the four tracks occupied with a Class 101 Metro-Cammell DMU about to enter the Mound tunnel heading for Waverley station, as Class 47 No 1575 [later 47455] emerges with the morning Leeds–Dundee express and a Class 40 waits for the signal to clear before heading west. Today the lines are busier than ever but with growth of the bushes and installed fencing the location is nothing like as good it used to be. *Date: 29th May 1972.*

The sight of a Finsbury Park white cab Deltic emerging from the 490 yards long Carlton North tunnel at Edinburgh Waverley was nothing unusual. In this case the train is not an ECML express, but a shuttle service from Dunbar following the collapse of Penmanshiel tunnel on 17th March 1979. The tunnel, 732 yards long, was built in 1845-1846 and had been the location of a less serious incident in 1949 when some carriages caught fire injuring seven people. Unfortunately the collapse killed two workmen and as the ground was considered too unstable to repair the tunnel it was sealed up and a diversion constructed. Deltic No 55007 named 'Pinza' was allocated to Finsbury Park depot when new in June 1961 as D9007. Its last seven months in service were at York before withdrawal in December 1981. *Date 4th August 1979.*

The scenery on the 392 miles of the ECML from London Kings Cross to Edinburgh Waverley is pleasant if unspectacular, except for the few miles around Berwick-upon-Tweed when it follows the North Sea coastline. The best section is north of Berwick, a distance of only six miles. Class 25 No 25226 is passing along the cliff tops with the 17.10 commuter service from Edinburgh Waverley. No 25226 was new as D7576 in November 1963 and lasted in service until June 1985. *Date 28th June 1976*

By the time this picture was taken Dumfries had lost its importance as a main railway centre. The fine station opened in 1859 and still survives, but the lines other than the Carlisle–Glasgow route have gone. These were the ones to Stranrear, Lockerbie and Moniaive. There was a steam locomotive shed and through lines through the station. Class 47/4 No 47523 is shown calling at the station on the 10.35 Stranraer to Euston, a service which no longer exists. No 47523 entered service numbered D1106 on 25th November 1966 and allocated to York. It spent nearly all its time allocated to ECML depots until in 1988 it moved to Stratford. By May 1998 it was carrying an unofficial name 'Railfreight'. Withdrawal was on 12th December 1998. *Date: 9th June 1983.*

The West Riding Branch of the RCTS ran a farewell to the Waverley route tour on the last day of operation. The tour is seen at Riccarton Junction which was possibly the most isolated and remote station on the BR

network. It had no road access until one was opened by the Forestry Commission long after the line had closed. A line across the Border Country used to leave from here to Hexham but lost its services on 15th October 1956. The RCTS had managed to get BR to provide a Deltic for the tour, which back in 1969 was not easy as the class was fully occupied on East Coast main line work. There was a light covering of snow which added interest to the photographic stop. The last train was the up St Pancras sleeper which ran later in the day and got into difficulties at Newcastleton when objectors to the closure apparently obstructed the level crossing gates and the police had to be called. *Date: 5th January 1969.*

North Eastern Region

After a perfect day of photography the sun is setting at Spittal just over a mile south of the Royal Border Bridge at Berwick-upon-Tweed. Class 47/4 No 47518 is accelerating hard as it gets the afternoon Aberdeen–Doncaster train up to line speed. No 47518 spent a good proportion of its career working ECML services. It was new in August 1966 numbered D1101 and eventually withdrawn in November 1991. *Date 10th June 1978.*

King Edward Bridge South Junction at Bensham on the south side of the Tyne near Gateshead sees class 40 No 40049 heading a summer Saturdays only Newcastle to Yarmouth train. The lines on the right pass under the ECML and head for Blaydon. No 40049 was allocated new to Gateshead as D249 in November 1959 and spent virtually all its time on the region until withdrawn in January 1983. *Date 6th August 1977.*

This is a view of the elegant Victoria viaduct on the Leamside line in the North East. Closure came in 1991 and it is recorded that the last train over it was in 1993, which was an engineers' train. Over the past 10 years the track has been removed, the final sections going in 2013. This is in spite of many investigations into the possible reopening of the line. Network Rail has apparently given an undertaking that no land will be sold and no bridges removed. The 11.45 diverted Newcastle–Liverpool express headed by class 47 No 47423 is seen heading south. By this date diversions were the main use for the line. The viaduct carries the line over the River Wear at a height of 135 feet. There are two arches of 100 feet, the other two being 160 feet and 144 feet. The line left the ECML at Tursdale and rejoined it at Pelaw. No 47423 was an Eastern Region locomotive when new in July 1963, eventually being withdrawn in August 1992. *Date 29th February 1989.*

This picture has been included to show the Transporter bridge rather than the class 101 DMU heading eastwards. It was opened in 1911 and officially known as the Tees Transporter Bridge. It is also called the Middlesbrough Transporter and locally as the 'Tranny'. It connects Middlesbrough on the south side with Port Clarence on the north. The structure was damaged by a bomb in World War 2 but it was repaired. It is a Grade II listed structure. The statistics are 850 feet in overall length and 590 feet between the towers, making it the longest working transporter bridge in the world. The gondola can take 200 people and nine cars, and the crossing takes 90 seconds. It has had major refurbishment work which involved its closure but it is now back in service. *Date 18th August 1984.*

This picture was taken at Battersby where the lines from Whitby and Middlesbrough join so that trains using the Esk Valley line now reverse. In the past, two other lines used to continue from here, one to Rosedale which closed in 1928 and the other to Picton. The latter lost its passenger services in 1954 and goods traffic in 1958. A Class 101 Metro-Cammell DMU is seen leaving past the signal box. *Date 28th June 1975.*

Class 55 Deltic No 55005 rounds the sweeping curve just north of York at Clifton before accelerating to its 100mph maximum on the ECML racing ground to the north. It is the point where the York avoiding line splits from the main line and is to the right of the picture. Mostly out of view are the buildings of the old York Carriage and wagon works. No 55005 'The Prince of Wales's Own Regiment of Yorkshire' was new to Gateshead depot in February 1961 where it remained until transferring to York in 1979 before being withdrawn in February 1981. It is heading a Kings Cross–Newcastle express. *Date 26th May 1978.*

Dringhouses Yard was situated at the south end of York on the east side of the main lines. Class 55 Deltic No 55004 'Queen's Own Highlander' is passing with the 12.40 Edinburgh Waverley to Kings Cross. A Class 37 and Class 08 shunter are also seen. All evidence of the yard has now vanished and an upmarket housing development has been built on the site. No 55004 was allocated to Haymarket depot when it entered service in May 1961. Like all members of the class it stayed at one depot during its career except for the last 21 months when it was at York before withdrawal in October 1981. During this latter period it was frequently used on Trans Pennine services to Liverpool along with other members of the class. *Date 29th April 1977.*

This view of the Selby swing bridge was taken from the control room on the top of the bridge. A Class 110 Birmingham Railway Carriage and Wagon Company 'Calder Valley' unit, as they were known, is shown heading north. The station can be seen in the background. The first railway bridge was built in 1840 for the Hull and Selby railway. This was replaced in 1891 by the present one, built by Nelson and Co and the Cleveland Bridge company. The bridge is still well used and had major work done on it in 2014.
Date 20th September 1983.

After the HSTs had taken over many of the ECML workings, the Deltics were frequently used on the Hull services. The Pullman services were replaced by trains named Executives. In summer 1978 the Hull Executive was launched. It departed at 06.50 am and returned from Kings Cross at 16.42. It was hauled by a mixture of Deltics and class 47s. The following year the down train was retimed to average 91.3mph to its first stop at Retford, making it the fastest locomotive hauled train in the country and producing some memorable performances by the Deltics. No 55021 'Argyll & Sutherland Highlander' is shown departing Hull station with a familiar Deltic exhaust on the 12.45 to Kings Cross. This was the last Deltic to be built, entering service in May 1962 at Haymarket Depot. As with most other members of the class it was moved to York in May 1979 before withdrawal in December 1981. *Date 12th July 1979.*

The local Class 03 shunter was kept very busy at Scarborough on summer Saturdays in the 1980s. At this time No 03089 was sub-shedded there from York. Class 31/1 No 31203 is in the background on an excursion. The station opened in 1845 and its claim to fame is that it has the longest station bench seat in the world at 158 yards long. It is clearly seen in the background. No 03089 had a 204hp Gardner engine and was new in May 1960, being taken out of use in 1987 before being preserved. *Date 23rd July 1980.*

Goole docks were developed from the mid-1820s supporting a community of 450. Today the town's population is in excess of 18,000. Originally it was built primarily to trans-ship coal from the Knottingley area, which was transported to Goole via the Aire and Calder canal. It is about 45 miles from the North Sea and today it can handle around three millions tons of goods, mainly timber. Class 08 No 08510 is seen from the road bridge on the west side of the docks. It was one of the 964 Class 08s constructed and it entered service in May 1958, numbered D3672. It was withdrawn in September 2008. *Date 9th September 1999.*

Even back when this picture was taken 36 years ago, locomotive hauled trains through Harrogate were thin on the ground. This was a troop train which had come over the Settle & Carlisle line from Scotland with personnel going to Catterick camp The locomotives ran round and are seen passing the 'Stray' just outside the station with the empty stock heading in the Leeds direction. The locomotives are Class 25/0s, Nos 25056 and 25060, both entering service in June 1963 numbered D5206 and D5210 respectively. Withdrawal for No 25056 was in August 1982 and for 25060 December 1985.
Date 30th July 1980.

After the closure of Leeds Central station on 1st May 1967, traffic was diverted to Leeds City station. The station has had several alterations to the track layouts as well as the rebuilding to cope with the ever increasing traffic. It is now known as plain Leeds. Class 47/4 No 47417 is seen coupled to an InterCity DVT and Mk4 coaches with Class 91 No 91008 electric at the rear. Diversions were in operation for Kings Cross trains on this date hence the use of the class 47. No 47417 was new in April 1963 as No D1516 and was withdrawn in 1992 after a period in store. It then passed into preservation and is currently at Butterley undergoing a complete restoration. *Date 18th November 1990.*

Class 37s were not often seen in the Leeds area in the latter 1970s and 1980s, but the 09.58 Weymouth–Leeds on this date had No 37127 in charge. It is passing though the Leeds suburbs at Hunslet on the old Midland Railway main line. It entered service in May 1963 on the Western Region as D6827. It was renumbered 37370 in July 1988 but suffered a main generator flash-over in 1990 and was stored for component recovery. However it was repaired. It was withdrawn in June 2005. *Date 18th June 1979.*

The background to this picture, taken from Pepper Road at Hunslet near Leeds and showing Class 25/0 No 25286 hauling some carflats on the up line, has kept changing since the end of the steam era in 1967. At the time of this picture the goods sidings were still used, but in due course the sidings area was used as a ballast collection centre. This then changed to the storage of freightliner containers until it was taken over by Freightliner and built its main diesel depot (known as Midland Road) which is still in use. No 25286 was new in November 1965 and was renumbered 25905 in November 1985. Withdrawal came in September 1986 but it was not scrapped for another four years. *Date 18th October 1979.*

The railways arrived in Castleford on 1st July 1840 and it still has a passenger service. Diversions were in operation on this Sunday as a Hull to Manchester train passes, formed by a Class 123 ex InterCity unit built in Swindon works in 1963. The fine array of signals has long since passed into history. These units were used in their final years on the Manchester–Sheffield–Cleethorpes route until Class 31s took over. All had been taken out of service by the summer of 1984. *Date 22nd May 1983.*

At the summit of the climb out of Leeds on the Wakefield Westgate route is the 297yards long Ardsley tunnel. Back in the latter 1970s the lupins on the embankment produced a very colourful sight. The 13.30 from Leeds to Kings Cross headed by class 47/4 No 47541 is seen passing. No 47541 has had an interesting career which it started with the number D1755 in August 1964. It was later allocated the number 47161 but this was never applied, receiving 47541 in November 1974 and eventually 47773 in December 1993. It received the name 'The Queen Mother' in October 1982. This was replaced in 1994 by 'Reservist' and the 'Queen Mother' nameplates were reapplied at Toton in August 2002. It can still be seen working on the network and is based at Tyseley. *Date 20th June 1978.*

Just to the east of the former Healey Mills marshalling yards near Wakefield is this impressive cutting at Horbury. When originally built as a two-track railway this part was in a tunnel, but it was opened out when the Lancashire and Yorkshire Railway expanded it to four tracks. Local Healey Mills yard shunter Class 08 No 08707 is shown passing through the cutting hauling a nuclear flask en route to the then Bombardier works a mile down the line for repair. The works were originally those of Charles Roberts, established in 1856 and taken over by Procor in 1974, then by Bombardier in 1990, ultimately closing in 2005. In its latter years the works constructed the bodies for the Class 60 locomotives and before it closed it was involved with some of the Virgin Class 220 and 221 Voyagers. *Date 23rd April 1990.*

The snow came in early December in 1976 at Wakefield. Class 46 No 46023 is passing the site of the once large ex Lancashire and Yorkshire Railway steam engine shed (coded 25A, then 56A) but which closed in 1967. Back in the early 1950s it had an allocation of over 120 locomotives which included around 60 WD 2-8-0s. The train is a cross country service from Leeds which had called at Wakefield Westgate before taking the spur at Oakenshaw to join the ex-Midland main line. No 46023 was new in March 1962, numbered D160 and allocated to Derby. It was allocated at various times to the LM, NE and Western regions. It was withdrawn in December 1983 and sent to the Derby Technical Centre where it was given the number 97402, but this was never applied. It was then broken up at Crewe Basford Hall in April 1994. *Date 3rd December 1976.*

Batley Carr between Dewsbury and Batley is the location for this picture of 2x2 car DMUs with a class 108 leading, working a Huddersfield to Leeds stopping service. Just to the right of the picture at a lower level was situated the ex-Great Northern Line into Dewsbury. The Class 108 DMUs were introduced in 1958 as two, three and four car sets. The final vehicle was taken out of traffic in 1993. *Date 1st August 1975.*

Clayton West was at the end of a 3½ mile branch which left the Huddersfield to Penistone line at Clayton West junction, just past Shepley station. There was a station opened in 1879 with passenger services lasting until 24th January 1983. There was also Park Mill colliery which at the time of this picture was served by a daily train from Healey Mills. All coal traffic ceased on the branch in July 1982, which included the other colliery at Skelmanthorpe named Emley Moor. The track bed and station area has now been taken over by the Kirklees Light Railway, a narrow gauge operation which is flourishing. The locomotive shunting the coal wagons is class 37/0 No 37040, then allocated to Healey Mills. It was new in June 1962 and not withdrawn until June 2005. *Date 5th August 1977.*

Left Huddersfield station was opened on 3rd August 1847 and is well known for its fine architecture. This view is taken from above the entrance to the 696-yards long Huddersfield tunnel which starts at the platform (west) end. Class 45/1 No 45146 is in platform 4 heading a York–Llandudno train. Today normally all up trains use the platform to the right unless there is a problem. No 45146 was new to Derby in April 1962 and numbered D66. It was selected for the fitting of Electric Train Heating in 1974. After it was withdrawn it saw further use at the Railway Technical Centre and was not scrapped until April 1992. *Date 9th August 1986.*

About a month before services were withdrawn a Class 101 DMU arrives at Clayton West with a service from Huddersfield. In the background can be seen the famous Emley Moor transmitting mast. At 1084 feet it is the tallest free-standing structure in the United Kingdom, and is grade II listed. There was a 443ft structure in 1956, but this was replaced by a 1266ft mast of tubular construction supported by guy ropes. On 19th March 1969 the force of the wind and the weight of ice caused a spectacular collapse. The new mast was in operation by 1971. *Date 14th November 1982.*

On the same day as the previous picture a class 101 DMU enters a very dilapidated Penistone station, on a Huddersfield–Sheffield service via Barnsley. The station at Penistone opened in 1845 but it was not until 1850 that the Lancashire and Yorkshire services started from Huddersfield. The present station dates from 1874. The line was threatened with closure but managed to survive after rationalisation of the tracks. It now has an hourly service in each direction, but with the single sections of track it is difficult to run any additional trains. Traffic is booming and the station has been much improved. *Date 14th November 1982.*

Paddock cutting is situated about 1½ miles to the west of Huddersfield on the main line to Standedge, which is on a 1 in 105 gradient to Marsden. It originally had four tracks but these were reduced to two many years ago. Double headed Class 25s on passenger workings by the 1980s over this route were not common. On this date a summer Saturdays only Scarborough to Manchester service has Nos 25221 and 25271 in charge. No 25221 entered service as D7571 in October 1963 while No 25271 arrived in August 1966 numbered D7621. Twenty-seven months separated their withdrawal dates, 25221 going in January 1984 and 25271 in October 1981. *Date 5th September 1981.*

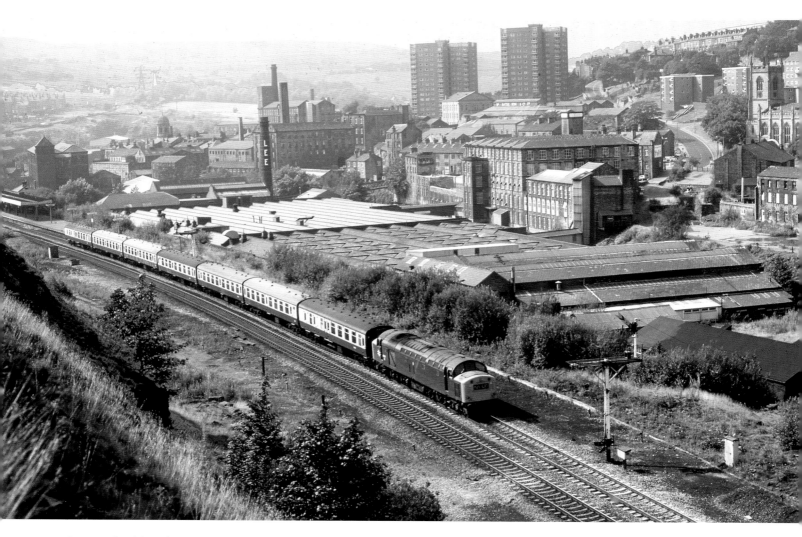

A scene looking down on Sowerby Bridge and the Calder Valley with a summer Saturdays only 12.00 Blackpool to Bradford Exchange leaving, headed by Class 40 No 40197. The station was opened in 1840 and is still in use today. The branch to Rishworth started here from the bottom side of the picture, but lost its passenger services in 1929, although the branch remained open for goods traffic until 1953. Class 40 No 40197 entered service numbered D397 in July 1962 and was withdrawn in September 1983. *Date 21st August 1976.*

Class 47/3 No 47357 is not long out of works as it heads the famous Heaton to Manchester Red Bank empty newspaper van train past the site of Elland station. The original station opened in 1841 but was resited in 1865 by 200 yards and then closed in 1962. Talks have been ongoing for some time about a reopening. In the background is Elland power station which was demolished some time ago and the signal box has also now gone. No 47357 was one of the 81 members of the class with no train heating supply (these were renumbered from 47301 onwards) and was new in June 1965 as D1876. It received the name 'The Permanent Way Institution' in June 1992, the plates being removed in 1995. It was officially withdrawn in 2001 although it had been out of use since 1996. This was a Sunday working when the train was much shorter. In the week it loaded to around 22 vans which in steam days meant it was always double headed by a wide variety of classes.
Date 23rd October 1983.

This vantage point gives a panoramic view of Brighouse in West Yorkshire. The open space behind the train was where the once extensive marshalling yard was situated. In the foreground there used to be two more main line tracks. Brighouse was where the main line used to go from four to two tracks up the Calder Valley. The marshalling yard site remained empty for many years but is now filled with industrial units. Class 37/0 No 37120 is heading east on a summer Saturdays extra from Blackpool to Sheffield. At this time, this summer train was the only one in the area to usually produce a class 37 during the year. No 37120 was numbered D6820 when new in March 1963. It was renumbered to 37887 in 1988 and named 'Castell Caerffili/Caerphilly Castle' in 1992. Stored in 1999, it was not finally withdrawn until August 2007. *Date 24th July 1976.*

Right St Dunstans station was operated by the Great Northern Railway and the Lancashire & Yorkshire Railway in 1878 and closed in 1952. It was about a mile out of Bradford Exchange station, on a very tight curve on a 1 in 50 gradient, which over the years produced plenty of problems. Generally today the DMUs which monopolise the services, together with the rail head treatment trains used in the autumn, solve any potential leaf-fall problems. St Dunstans was part of a triangle with the old Great Northern lines to Queensbury, Keighley, Halifax and Laisterdyke. The carriage sidings were also here and the ex Lancashire and Yorkshire line to Halifax left at Hall Lane just before the station. Deltic No 55020 'Nimbus' is rounding the curve on the 11.55 from Exchange to Kings Cross. No 55020 went new to Finsbury Park depot in February 1962 where it stayed for its entire career. This and No 55001 'St Paddy' became the first of the famous class to be scrapped. They were taken out of use between January 1980 and January 1982, mainly due to a shortage of spare power units. Both were withdrawn in January 1980 and cut up at Doncaster BREL works.
Date 18th May 1977.

Guiseley Junction at Shipley used to have a fine array of signals. Class 101 DMU in the short lived white and blue livery is coming off the branch from Guiseley on to the main line as another unit is heading for Leeds. Shipley is still a busy centre with the triangle of lines to Bradford Forster Square, Skipton and Leeds as well as the branch to Guiseley and Ilkley. The railways arrived in Shipley in 1846 but the station was moved by a quarter of a mile in 1849. The route is now electrified and operates an excellent service along the Aire valley and to Ilkley. *Date 22nd July 1979.*

Eastern Region

Prior to the electrification of the ECML the approach to Bridge Junction about a mile south of Doncaster station was an excellent vantage point to photograph down trains. Deltic No 55005 'The Prince of Wales's Own Regiment of Yorkshire' sweeps round the curve at the head of the midday Kings Cross to Aberdeen express. In the distance to the left can be seen where the old steam shed once existed and where the diesel depot stands. Nearer to the camera on the left is where the depot for the new IEP trains is currently being built. No 55005 has already featured on page 32 where its history was given. *Date 18th June 1978.*

A group of locomotives passes through the up centre road at Doncaster station. Class 31/1 No 31156 is leading class 47/4s Nos 47417 and 47433. They were heading for the depot for servicing. No 31156 entered service in December 1959 numbered D5574 and was withdrawn in 1992. *Date 19th June 1978.*

The sidings alongside the former Royal Mail terminal at Decoy about two miles south of Doncaster station have been a concentration centre for MGR traffic for many years. Class 47/0 No 47223 is seen on a train about to head north. The sidings are still used but the number of trains has recently declined. No 47223 entered service in May 1965 numbered D1873. It became part of the Petroleum sector fleet and named 'British Petroleum' in August 1990. It was officially withdrawn in May 2000 after a six year period in store for component recovery. *Date 23rd January 1985.*

A massive rationalisation of the freight yards in the Sheffield and Rotherham areas in the early 1960s resulted in the construction of the Tinsley Marshalling Yard in 1965. After opening, it was handling 3000 wagons per day, but even as early as the 1970s traffic started to decline. There were eleven reception sidings which served fifty sorting sidings via automated hump shunting. As the standard class 08 shunters were not powerful enough for the work, a dedicated class of three master and slave shunters were designed and classed 13s. These were formed from two Class 08s. No 13003 is seen near the hump between duties. As part of the yard operation, a purpose-built locomotive depot was incorporated into the project. The pattern of traffic altered dramatically in the early 1980s resulting in the yard closing in 1984, although the locomotive depot continued until 1998. Currently steel traffic still calls on most days for Outokumpo Steel. The class 13s entered service between May and July 1965. No 13002 was withdrawn in 1981. Nos 13001 and 13003 lasted until 1985.
Date 29th July 1976.

This is Hatfield and Stainforth where the first station opened in 1866. A new station was opened in September 1992. It is situated to the east of Doncaster, the station being about a mile from where the line splits, one route going to Scunthorpe and the other to Goole. Two Class 31/1s, Nos 31227 and 31235 are heading west with an empty coke train from Scunthorpe. In the background can be seen the colliery, which was rail connected but closed in 2015 after a difficult previous 10 years involving several organisations, with some going into receivership. A massive landslip from the colliery in February 2013 resulted in the four tracks of the line being completely closed until July. No 31227 was new as D5653 in September 1960 and withdrawn in 1988. No 31235 entered service in October 1960 numbered D5662. It is now owned by Harry Needle but stored on the Mid-Norfolk Railway. *Date 15th April 1981.*

The magnificent Lincoln Cathedral (also known as St Mary's Cathedral) dominates the skyline of this picture as it does for miles around the flat countryside. Construction started in 1088 and continued for centuries during which there were some major collapses of the structure. It is the third largest cathedral in the UK. The swans in the river are taking little notice of Class 31/4 No 31431 passing with the summer Saturdays only 13.10 from Skegness to Sheffield. No 31431 entered service in January 1961 on the Eastern Region numbered D5681. It received the number 31253 in 1974 followed by 31431 in 1983 when it was fitted with ETH. In 1990 it was transferred to the Departmental sector and became No 31531. It was stored in 1995, eventually being withdrawn in February 2000, but not scrapped until July 2003. *Date 28th May 1988.*

Trade at Grimsby dated back to medieval times, with the start of dock development as far back as 1700. Expansion took place in 1840 due to the Manchester, Sheffield and Lincolnshire Railway, and in the 1880s coal and timber were the main traffic. From 1970, cars have been one of the main imports. The fishing industry developed from 1857, with Grimsby becoming one of the main fishing ports in the country until the industry collapsed in 1970. An unidentified class 08 can be seen in the docks. *Date 8th May 1992.*

In the days of through services from Kings Cross to Cleethorpes, Class 47/4 No 47409 is calling at Barnetby with the 08.05 from Kings Cross. The station opened here in 1848. The line became very busy with import traffic from Immingham and Grimsby docks as well as passenger services from Cleethorpes. Today it is still busy but with some of the coal traffic starting to be replaced by biomass trains. No 47409 was new to the Eastern Region in January 1963 numbered D1508. It was named 'David Lloyd George 'in 1985. After fire damage at Montrose, it was withdrawn in August 1986. *Date 12th June 1981.*

Heckington is on the Sleaford–Boston–Skegness line. The station opened in 1859 and is still in use. The Windmill dominates the skyline by the station. It was built in 1830 and ceased work in 1946. It was bought by the Kesteven Council in 1953 and after a major restoration in 2004 has become the only eight-sailed working windmill in the country. Class 31/1 No 31248 is passing the station on a summer Saturday working to Skegness. No 31248 was new to the Eastern Region in December 1960 and numbered D5676. It was stored in 1993 but not scrapped until March 2000. *Date 14th July 1979.*

Stoke Tunnel on the East Coast Main line is just over 100 miles from Kings Cross and 880 yards long. The 15 miles from Tallington to the summit of Stoke bank just before the tunnel was mainly at gradients of 1 in 200 with the final three miles at 1 in 178. In the steam era this section of line produced some remarkable performances by the Gresley Pacifics and other classes, and of course the world's steam speed record in the up direction. Deltic No 55018 'Ballymoss' bursts out of the tunnel at the head of the 13.00 Kings Cross to Edinburgh Waverley. No 55018 was allocated to Finsbury Park depot from new in November 1961, numbered D9018. It spent its last five months allocated to York before withdrawal in October 1981. *Date 27th May 1978.*

This picture was taken at Peterborough from the road bridge just north of the station before the electrification of the line. Class 31/1 No 31253 is shown leaving the station working hard with the 12.30 Yarmouth to Birmingham New Street train. Details of No 31253 are given on page 54 when it had been numbered 31431. *Date 12th September 1981.*

Finsbury Park depot in north London was the first purpose built main line diesel depot to be opened in the UK. It was commissioned in April 1960, primarily to provide the locomotives to work the East Coast main line expresses out of Kings Cross. It is always associated with the famous Deltic Class 55s, its fleet being named after racehorses carrying on the tradition of the LNER with its Class A3 pacifics. With the introduction of the HSTs the depot was downgraded in 1981 and finally closed in October 1983. The site is now covered with flats. Two of the Finsbury Park Deltics – No 55009 'Alycidon' and No 55015 'Tulyar' – together with a Class 46 are receiving attention. Both spent nearly all their time allocated here, No 55009 arriving in July 1961 followed by 55015 three months later. Happily both are now in the care of the Deltic Preservation Society. No 55009 is currently in full working order and 55015 is undergoing a lengthy major restoration. *Date 2nd November 1981.*

The Deltics dominated the fast ECML passenger services for 20 years. There were periods when their availability was poor and the class 47s did a lot of deputising. Seen from above Gasworks tunnel (528 yards) and before the rationalisation of the trackwork and the electrification, No 55020 'Nimbus' is leaving the station on the 11.25am to Leeds. On the right is the stabling point yard where locomotives were refuelled unless they needed attention at Finsbury Park depot. In the background is St Pancras station. No 55020 was one of the first two of the class to be withdrawn in January 1980 along with 55001 'St Paddy'. It was new to the 'Park' in February 1962. *Date 10th July 1976.*

Anglia Region

The silver roof on class 47/4 No 47482 indicates it was allocated to Stratford depot in east London at this time. It is shown climbing the short 1 in 70 gradient between Liverpool Street station and Bethnal Green heading the 14.10 to Cambridge. No 47482 was new in December 1964 to the Western Region, numbered D1636. It was allocated to several regions during its career which ended in October 1993. *Date 19th March 1985.*

Class 31/1 No 31110 (a class nicknamed skinheads as they were not fitted with route indicator boxes on the cabs) passes Belstead Summit between Ipswich and Manningtree on a permanent way train. The bank is at 1 in 157 for just under two miles on the south side and varies on the north side between 1 in 120 and 1 in 200. No 31110 was new to Norwich as D5528 in April 1959 and was named 'Traction Magazine' in 1999. After periods in store between 1996. It was withdrawn in February 2001 and scrapped in April 2007. *Date 13th April 1984.*

Class 47/4 No 47568 emerges from the 361 yards long Ipswich Tunnel [also called Stoke Tunnel] heading a Norwich to Liverpool Street express. Ipswich station is at the other end of the tunnel. No 47568 carried several numbers starting with D1626 when new in October 1964; 47045 followed in 1974, then 47568 in 1980 and finally 47726 in 1995 when it became part of the RES fleet. It carried the name 'Royal Engineers Postal & Courier Services' in 1990 and was renamed 'Royal Logistics Corps Postal & Courier Services' in 1993. It received another name in 1995 'Manchester Airport Progress'. It was withdrawn in 2002 but not scrapped until 2007. *Date 14th April 1984.*

Seen from above Ipswich Tunnel looking south, Class 47/3 No 47363 with Stratford depot silver roof is heading a down container train towards the station. No 47363 was one of the 81 members of the class built without train heating and was new as D1882 in July 1965. It was named 'Billingham Enterprise' in 1985 and renumbered to 47385 in 1994 but reverted to 47363 in 1995. It was stored in 1999 and sold to Fragonset Railways in 2001, arriving at Carnforth for storage in 2002. It was eventually scrapped in March 2010. *Date 13th April 1984.*

Looking down on Ipswich station and to the north, a Norwich to Liverpool Street express is shown about to leave. The original station at Ipswich opened in 1846 as a terminus. The station was replaced in 1860 as a through station. Stratford-allocated class 47/4 No 47585 (named 'County of Cambridgeshire' in 1979) is at the head of the train. It entered service numbered D1779 in October 1964 and was renumbered to 47184 in 1974, then 47585 in 1981 and finally 47757 in April 1994. It was first stored in 1988 and withdrawn in 1992. Reinstatement came in January 1994 and it was named 'Restitution' in the following year. It was renamed again to 'Capability Brown' in 2003. Withdrawal came in July 2005. *Date 12th April 1984.*

Parkeston Quay (now called Harwich International Port) shows Class 31/1 No 31238 waiting for its next duty out of the yard as No 31419 leaves with a service for Peterborough and Birmingham. The funnel of one of the ferries towers above the buildings, having brought passengers across the North Sea with a connecting train service to Liverpool Street station in London. No 31238 entered service at March in November 1960 numbered D5665. A period of storage came in 1991 and is believed to have been cut up in 1999 without an official withdrawal date. No 31419 was one of the class to be fitted with ETH. It was new in May 1961 to Stratford depot as D5697 and was renumbered first to 31267 and then 31419 in 1982. It entered the department fleet and became 31519 in 1990. It was withdrawn in August 1999. *Date 14th April 1984.*

At one time Great Yarmouth had three separate stations. Only one now remains as shown here and is Yarmouth Vauxhall. It was originally called Vauxhall and opened in 1844. Class 37/0 No 37109 is departing on a summer Saturdays only 09.15 to Newcastle. No 37109 was new as D6809 in February 1963 and stored in 2001, eventually passing into preservation. *Date 25th August 1979.*

This picture was taken at King's Lynn which is just over 96 miles from London. The railways arrived here in 1846 and the original station was replaced by the current one in 1871. There are also railways into the docks. Class 37/0 No 37092 was new to Gateshead depot in February 1963 numbered D6792. It was scrapped in 2001 having been withdrawn the previous year. *Date 25th August 1979.*

This picture taken at Norwich from the bridge just outside the station shows two class 25/0s Nos 25158 and 25101 leaving with a summer Saturday service to Yarmouth. The station originally opened in May 1844 but was moved in 1866. The lines were electrified in 1986. It is 124 miles from Liverpool Street via Cambridge and 114 miles via Ipswich. No 25158 was new in November 1964 numbered D7508 and 25101 entered service in February 1964 as D5251. Both were withdrawn in 1983. *Date 25th August 1979.*

Southern Region

Class 33/0 No 33002 is at the buffer stops inside Waterloo station, which was opened in 1848. It has just brought the empty Pullman coaches in, which were to form a special called the Bournemouth Belle. The last time the Bournemouth Belle ran as a titled train was in July 1967. No 33002 was the second of the class to enter traffic in February 1960 and numbered D6501. It received the name 'Sea King' in November 1991 until the plates were removed in 1996 when it went into store. It was withdrawn in 1997 but sold that year to Harry Needle who in turn sold it to Direct Rail Services, who reinstated it in June 2001. It is now preserved. *Date 21st June 1986.*

Class 33/1 No 33101 has just passed through Clapham Junction station heading the 10.10 from Waterloo to Salisbury. The station dates from 1863. The four tracks seen in the photograph are the ex-LSWR ones to Woking and beyond. Behind the bridge are the extensive carriage sidings. No 33101 was new in June 1960 numbered D6511 and was one of the class to be converted for push-pull working, then being classified as 33/1. It was withdrawn in May 1993 and eventually scrapped in 1997. *Date 15th April 1989.*

The footbridge just to the West of Woking station is an excellent location to see traffic on both the Basingstoke and Portsmouth lines. The railway arrived here in 1838 and it is still a very busy place. Class 33/0s Nos 33006 and 33004 are leaving the yard with a down tank train. They entered service in April and March 1960 respectively, numbered D6504 and D6506. They were both withdrawn in 1991. *Date 17th August 1988.*

There is a large permanent way depot at Woking which can be seen in the background of this picture. Class 09 No 09004 was based here at the time the picture was taken and is seen with some loaded ballast wagons heading along the Portsmouth line before shunting them into the sidings on the right. No 09004 was new as D3668 to the Southern Region in February 1959 where it spent its entire career until withdrawn in 1999 and sold for preservation in 2000. *Date 17th August 1988.*

This impressive view of Brighton can be had from a footpath along the top of a very high embankment just outside the station which is called Lovers Walk. In the yard are a selection of locomotives, Class 33 Nos 33023, 33052 and 33021 along with Class 73 Nos 73101 and 73104. The line just visible in the foreground goes along the coast to Portsmouth and Southampton; in the middle is the main line to London and the one branching off to the right goes to Lewes. London Road viaduct can just be seen, as the line climbs up Falmer Bank. *Date 11th August 1979.*

The main line was closed over this weekend between Winchester and Basingstoke resulting in the class 33s being out in force dragging the EMUs around on the then non-electrified coast route. No 33101 is seen again (see page 67) and this time is hauling a down train over Wallington viaduct near Fareham.
Date 28th February 1987.

The top of the multi-storey car park at Eastleigh provides an excellent point to view all the activity on the Southampton–Waterloo main as well as the one to Portsmouth. It also provides a point where with a pair of binoculars you can identify most of the items outside the works. Class 33/1 No 33116 is approaching the station with an EMU from Portsmouth. Another 33 sets off down the Portsmouth line and in the works yard two Class 33s can be seen as well as the Class 07 works shunter. The old steam shed and diesel depot was behind all the works buildings. No 33116 entered service on the Southern Region in December 1960. In its latter years it became a bit of a celebrity after it was named 'Hertfordshire Rail Tours' in December 1993. It even worked as far as Inverness on a special. It was involved in an accident in August 1998 and withdrawn. It then passed into preservation. *Date 28th February 1987.*

Class 33/0 No 33015 is emerging from the 443-yards long Fisherton Tunnel, about a mile east of Salisbury. It is working the 11.00 Waterloo to Exeter service. At the other end of the tunnel is Salisbury Tunnel Junction where the line to Eastleigh and Southampton leaves the main line to Waterloo. No 33015 went to Hither Green depot when new in September 1960 numbered D6523. Withdrawal came in July 1989 due to fire damage. It was eventually scrapped in December 1990. *Date 1st June 1979.*

The present day Bournemouth Central station with its fine overall roof opened in 1885. Class 33/1 No 33104 is arriving with an up boat train from Weymouth. In the days of steam the engine shed yard used to be in the background but has now become a car park, and the ring road bridge did not exist. No 33104 was another member of the class modified for push/pull working. It was new in July 1960 as D6516 and withdrawn in December 1985 after it ran into the back of an EMU which it had been sent to rescue on the 26th January 1985. *Date 20th July 1979.*

Class 33/0 No 33033 is working hard as it hauls a Poole to Newcastle relief through the woods as it climbs Parkstone Bank. It is a difficult three miles on the up line from Poole station, which is on a sharp curve and after a short section of level track the gradient becomes 1 in 60 for just over two miles to Branksome. Banking assistance in steam days was provided for heavy trains, but in the diesel days there was often a loco at the rear, usually as a way of returning it to Bournemouth or the carriage sidings on the Bournemouth West branch. Today the electrics handle it with ease. No 33033 was new in April 1961 and numbered D6551. From 1988 it kept being put into store and reinstated until finally withdrawn in May 1993. *Date 18th May 1979.*

Class 47/4 No 47446 is handling the Poole to Newcastle train with ease as it crosses the edge of Poole Park, climbing the 1 in 60 gradient mentioned in the previous picture. No 47446 was new to Tinsley depot in April 1964 numbered D1563. It received the unofficial name of 'Galtee More' (once carried by a Gresley A3 pacific) in December 1990. Withdrawal came in February 1992. *Date 20th July 1979.*

The closure of the Weymouth Quay branch has been opposed many times over the last decades. In days past it was busy with boat trains to France and the Channel Islands as well as freight. There have been no scheduled trains for 25 years except for specials. One of these was run by Hertfordshire Rail Tours on 10th December 1988 and hauled in top and tail mode by class 33/1s Nos 33113 and 33114. The special is seen on the quayside making very slow progress to the terminal. The passengers were not allowed to travel in the train but had the opportunity to see cars being bounced out of the way which were obstructing the line. The line has been out of use since 2009. No 33113 was one of the class fitted with push/pull for working the electric stock from Bournemouth to Weymouth. It was new in November 1960 numbered D6531 and after several periods in store was withdrawn in October 1992. No 33114 was new in November 1960 and numbered D6532. It was withdrawn in February 1993. *Date 10th December 1988.*

Western Region

Taken from a vantage point high above Ranelagh Yard outside Paddington station, where steam and diesels used to be turned and serviced, avoiding a trip to Old Oak Common shed/depot, is Class 47/4 No 47509 'Albion' leaving on the 14.05 to Oxford. 'Albion' was new in November 1966 and numbered D1953. It operated on the Western Region from 1973 to 1988 and was cut up at Bristol Bath Road in November 1995. *Date 13th July 1985.*

A special test train approaches Acton Yard on the up slow headed by Class 31/4s Nos 31413 and 31442. No 31413 was new in August 1961 as D5812. It was named 'The Severn Valley Railway' at Bewdley station on the SVR on 22nd April 1988. It received a modified livery which made it easily recognisable from the others. It retained the livery until withdrawn in May 1997 after several periods in and out of store from 1993. No 31442 went to the Eastern Region when it entered service in December 1960 numbered D5679. It carried the number 31251 from February 1974 until receiving ETH Equipment when it became 31442. Final withdrawal came in 1993. *Date 28th April 1989.*

This impressive view is not now obtainable due to the masts and wires being installed for electrification. Class 56 No 56042 is heading a down stone train. No 56042 was unique within the class as it was selected for development work for the new CP1 bogie design being developed by BREL (British Rail Engineering Ltd). No 56042 ran with these new bogies during its career. The design was eventually fitted to the class 58s. No 56042 entered service at Toton in 1979 but had been in use on test work for around a year. It suffered fire damage in 1983, was repaired and then went to the Railway Technical Centre at Derby. It returned to traffic for a short spell but was out of use at the end of 1989. It was officially withdrawn in September 1991 when the CP1 bogies were removed. *Date 6th August 1988.*

Class 50 No 50049 'Defiance' in shabby external condition is taking the up relief line away from Didcot heading a Birmingham to Paddington express. Didcot power station cooling towers can be seen in the background. It has recently been demolished, which unfortunately made headline news when there was a massive collapse of the main structure resulting in fatalities. No 50049 was new in December 1968, numbered D449 and allocated to Crewe for working the Scottish expresses until the electrification reached Glasgow. Like the rest of the class it was transferred to the Western Region when the electrics took over. It was renumbered to 50149 in 1987 and painted into Train load livery. Laira depot made modifications to it for it to be used on freight work. It was tested on china clay and stone workings, but the tests were not considered a success and in 1989 it was returned to its original condition. It was withdrawn in 1991 and passed into preservation. It has worked on the network quite frequently over the years. *Date 17th April 1982.*

The 10.30 Paddington to Plymouth is approaching Westbury station headed by Class 50 No 50042 'Triumph'. There is a triangle at the east end of Westbury station; the lines heading off on the left are for Bath and other locations. No 50042 entered service in October 1968 as D442 at Crewe to work the Scottish services northwards. It was withdrawn in October 1990 at Laira depot and eventually passed into preservation. *Date 14th September 1979.*

This fine location at the west end of Exeter St David's station has been a favourite with photographers for decades. The station opened on 1st May 1844 and is now the main station in the city. One of the 74 Class 52 'Western' diesel hydraulics, No 1049 'Western Monarch', is leaving with a down van train. With the British Railways Board's decision to concentrate on diesel electrics the Class 52s had short careers. No 1049 was new in December 1963, surviving until 1976 only. *Date 5th September 1975.*

The section of railway between Dawlish and Teignmouth is one of the most photographed in the UK. Here Class 52 No D1019 'Western Challenger' has just passed Dawlish station with a down evening freight on a fine September evening. This section of line is extremely vulnerable to the storms off the sea, and recently had to be closed for a lengthy period due to a major landslip just the other side of the station. D1019 was one of four members of the class which was not fitted for dual braking and was therefore a candidate for early withdrawal, which came in May 1973 after only ten years of service. *Date 1st September 1972.*

This location is Lipson Junction just over a mile to the east of Plymouth station and very close to Laira depot which is really the nerve centre of the railways in the west country. Class 47/4 No 47620 named 'Windsor Castle' is at the head of the 10.25 Birmingham New Street to Penzance express. The Class 118 DMU set No P460 in British Telecom livery can be seen to the right hand side. No 47620 had several identities and was eventually selected as one of the two 'Royal' Class 47s. It was numbered D1654 when new in January 1965. No 47070 followed in 1974 and then 47620 in 1984. It was named 'Windsor Castle' at Paddington on 26th July 1985. It was later renumbered to 47799 and renamed 'Prince Henry' and was in a dedicated pool for Royal train duties and painted in the royal livery. Prior to this it had been renumbered in August 1989 from 47620 to 47835. In late 2002 it could be seen on a variety of duties, even freight, after the Class 67s took over the royal workings. Not surprisingly it has been preserved. *Date 24th August 1985.*

256 miles from Paddington the railway crosses the 326 yards long St Germans viaduct, one of the many fine structures on the scenic but relatively slow line from Plymouth to Penzance. A Swindon built 'Cross Country' Class 120 DMU, now reduced to a two car set, is heading west on a local service from Plymouth. The class was introduced in October 1957 and remained in service until 1989. *Date 8th April 1980.*

Par station opened in 1859 and together with the goods yards at St Blazey and locomotive shed/depot rapidly developed into a very busy centre based on the china clay traffic. It is also the point where the branch to Newquay left the main line. The china clay traffic is now sadly very much reduced, but here we see from the road bridge immediately to the east of the station, ex-works Class 37/0 No 37299 is about to haul china clay wagons back into the yard at St Blazey, as there is no direct access to the yards for traffic coming from the west. At the other end of the train is Class 25/0 No 25207. The china clay traffic has used a wide variety of classes over the years including the diesel hydraulics. Currently the Class 66s cover what is needed. No 37299 was new in August 1965 numbered D6999. It became No 37299 in 1974 and after the fitting of ETH it was numbered 37426 and named 'Y Lein Fach/Vale of Rheidol'. It then initially joined the small fleet of 37/4s for working the Cambrian Coast services. It was withdrawn by EWS in February 2004. *Date 10th April 1980.*

Penzance is 306 miles from Paddington and the station was opened on 11th March 1852. The servicing depot is situated about a mile from Penzance station at Long Rock. Class 50 No 50049 'Defiance' is again seen in poor external condition ready to leave the station on the 10.21 to Leeds. Details about the locomotive have been given on page 76. *Date 9th October 1978.*

Severn Tunnel Junction station is on the South Wales main line and opened in December 1886. A large goods yard developed here, having its own steam shed and later a diesel depot. It was the place where cars were loaded to be taken through the tunnel. This service operated from 1924 to 1966 when the opening of the Severn Bridge made the service redundant. With the changing patterns of freight traffic the yards were closed on 12th October 1987. Class 118 DMU set No 480 is leaving the station heading for Newport. *Date 2nd March 1987.*

Just to the west of Newport station in South Wales are the new and old Hillfield tunnels. Class 33 No 33053 is emerging from the new tunnel and is about to call at the station with the 10.10 Cardiff to Portsmouth service. The Class 33s were regular performers on these services in the latter 1980s as well as the services from Cardiff to Crewe and North Wales. No 33053 was new, like the rest of the class, to the Southern Region in October 1961 where it was numbered D6571. It was withdrawn in February 1997 after periods in store and was sold to the Harry Needle company. *Date 4th August 1987.*

This scene was taken looking down on Parson Street junction, which is situated about two miles from Bristol Temple Meads station on the Taunton Line. The Portishead branch is leaving to the right and the Bristol

Railport depot can also be seen. A class 117 DMU is approaching the station, opened in August 1927, with a service from Weston-super-Mare. The Class 117s were built by the Pressed Steel Co in 1959-61 but most were withdrawn by the early 1990s. *Date 20th June 1987.*

This view of Bristol Temple Meads station is obtained from the road bridge at the west end of the station where Bath road steam shed and diesel depot was once situated. Class 47/4 No 47615 is seen removing the sleeping coaches off the overnight train from Glasgow Central. The train then continued to the West Country. In the background can be seen a class 33 on a Cardiff to Portsmouth service. To the left in the siding is preserved 'King' class steam engine No 6023 before restoration. No 47615 was new to Bath Road depot as D1929 in 1966. It became 47252 in 1974, 47615 in 1984 and finally 47747 in 1994 as part of the RES fleet. It was taken over by EWS and sold to Rivera Train in 2007 and on to DRS in 2011. It saw very little use and was broken up in June 2013. It also carried other names in its latter years. *Date 6th July 1985*

After over 100 years in use the timber viaduct that crosses the Mawddach estuary at Barmouth was in need of urgent repairs due to being attacked by woodworm. This resulted in the banning of locomotives over it. This initially created a problem for permanent way trains as there is no other rail connections north of Barmouth on the Cambrian coast line to Pwllheli. The solution was found in Class 128 single car DMUs. No 55995 is shown at Tywyn hauling a couple of ballast wagons on these PW duties. The bridge carries the single track, pedestrians and cyclists, currently without charge. Due to the cost of maintaining it for public use consideration is being given to closing the footpath. *Date 2nd September 1984.*

The station at Hereford opened in 1853. The town developed into an important railway centre with lines to Worcester, Shrewsbury, Cardiff, Gloucester and Brecon. Except for the latter two the others are still busy. It had a steam shed located on an avoiding line. A Class 120 DMU is leaving the south end of the station on a Birmingham to Cardiff service. *Date 1st October 1977.*

The 'Crewe Invader' tour organised by F&W Railtours provided a field day for Class 50 enthusiasts, giving them 646 miles in the day from Plymouth to Crewe and return, for a works open day. Laira depot rose to the occasion and turned out No 50008 in immaculate condition. The special is seen approaching Church Stretton on the outward journey. D408 was new to Crewe in March 1968 and was renumbered 50008 in 1974. It received the name 'Thunderer' in September 1978. Withdrawal came in June 1992 and it was sold to Pete Waterman in 1992. It is still in existence. *Date 22nd September 1979.*

Two Class 25/0s are seen just past Sutton Bridge junction at the start of the single track section on the outskirts of Shrewsbury. The train is a summer Saturdays Euston–Aberystwyth service. These workings, which the class performed until the late 1980s, became the last trains to have regular main line Class 25 haulage. Nos 25265 and 25287 are heading the train. No 25265 was new to the Scottish Region in May 1966 numbered D7615. No 25287 entered service at Tinsley depot in November 1965 as D7637 and was withdrawn in July 1976 after collision damage, but then reinstated the following September. It was withdrawn in December 1985 and cut up in 1987. *Date 18th August 1984*

This commanding view of Shrewsbury station is obtained from the Severn Bridge Junction signal box. Construction started in 1902 and it was completed in 1904. It has 180 levers, making it now the largest mechanical operated signal box in the world. Currently only about half the levers are in use, but two signalmen are needed to operate it. Class 47/4 No 47479 is leaving with the 16.34 through train to London Euston. These services were withdrawn but will be reinstated in the future. The imposing building in the background was the prison, which closed in March 2013. No 47479 was new to the Western Region in August 1964, numbered D1612, and named 'Track 29' on 27th July 1979. It was badly damaged at St Erth, Cornwall on 24th October 1992 and withdrawn the following December. *Date 18th August 1984.*

London Midland Region

The magnificent St Pancras train shed is seen to advantage in this picture of Class 45/1 No 45115 leaving with an 18.01 departure for Sheffield. This sight has now been consigned to history with the opening of the international station. The class 45s dominated the Midland Main Line services after the end of steam. Fifty members of the class were fitted with ETH equipment in the mid-1970s and these locomotives worked the services until the arrival of the HSTs in 1982. No 45115 was new in December 1960 numbered D81. It was renumbered 45115 in 1973 and continued in service until withdrawn in May 1988. *Date 6th May 1978.*

This is Kentish Town with a Class 127 DMU calling with a local service to St Pancras. The station is 1½ miles from St Pancras and was opened in 1868. The Class 127s were introduced in May 1959 and were built at Derby as four-car sets with Rolls-Royce engines. They were known as 'Bedpans' (Bedford to St Pancras) and their features made them incompatible with other units. They were only meant to be a stop gap measure prior to electrification of the Midland Main Line, but they lasted 24 years until the Class 317 EMUs entered service in 1983. *Date 21st May 1977.*

Six miles north of St Pancras is Brent Junction, where class 45/1 No 45140 is seen passing with a up Midland Main Line express. The A406 North Circular Road can be seen in the background on the bridge. No 45140 entered service at Derby when new as D102 in May 1961. It was withdrawn in March 1988 and scrapped in 1994. *Date 21st May 1977.*

An up express headed by class 45/1 No 45148 is passing Finedon Road signal box and the extensive Neilsons sidings. These are situated just north of Wellingborough station. Finedon once had a station, which opened in 1857 and closed in 1940. The old large steam shed was half a mile to the south towards the station on the up side. As was the case with most members of the Class 45s, it was allocated to Derby when new in December 1961. Originally numbered D130, it survived in service until February 1987 and was scrapped five years later. *Date 16th August 1980.*

Class 47/4 No 47514 has just arrived at Loughborough station with an up Midland Main Line express. The original station opened in 1840, but was replaced in 1872 to the north of the road bridge from where this picture was taken. In the background the famous 'Falcon' Brush works can be seen. This site originated back to 1889 and manufactured mainly electrical products. Involvement in railway work started in the late 1940s. In 1960, four thousand three hundred people were employed in the separate locomotive and carriage works activities. Many well known diesel and electric locomotives have been built here, and it is still involved in railway locomotive work today but on a very much reduced scale. No 47514 was new from the works in July 1967 numbered D1960. It became No 47514 in 1974 and then 47703 when allocated to the push/pull dedicated fleet for the Scottish Region. It has carried the following names: 'Saint Mungo', 'The Queen Mother', 'Lewis Carroll' and 'Hermes'. It was stored in March 1997 and sold to Fragonset Railways. Currently owned by Harry Needle, it is operational but not main line certified. *Date 29th May 1978.*

No 45127 is seen just to the north of Burton upon Trent station, accelerating towards Derby with an express for Newcastle. By this date the extensive sidings which had catered for the brewing industry had been removed and the tracks rationalised. No 45127 was numbered D87 when new in February 1961. Withdrawal came in May 1987. *Date 25th August 1980.*

Derby developed into one of the country's main railway centres after the railways arrived in 1839. The original station was opened but was quickly replaced by the station on the present site in 1840. Main lines currently radiate from it to Birmingham, Leicester and Sheffield and Nottingham. The Midland Railway established its main locomotive and carriage works here, building of rolling stock and refurbishment work being still carried out by Bombardier Transportation Ltd. The Railway technical centre was also based here, but the site was sold to Railway Vehicle Engineering Ltd [RVEL] who used it for storing and repairing locomotives and stock. It was sold again to US firm Loram in 2016. Class 25/0 No 25215 was built in the works in December 1965, emerging numbered D7565. It is approaching Derby on a summer Saturdays only Llandudno to Nottingham train, which would reverse at Derby. It was withdrawn in June 1983. *Date 5th August 1978.*

This location at Hasland just over a mile to the south of Chesterfield station allows the main feature of the town to be included in the picture, namely the crooked spire of the parish church completed in 1360. The church was struck by lightning in 1861 causing a fire which may have contributed to the spire twisting, although there are other explanations. It is twisted by 45 degrees and leans by 9 feet 5 inches. Class 45/0 No 45022 is shown heading south on the up fast line with a van train. It was new in February 1962 numbered D60 and named 'Lytham St Annes' in May 1964. Withdrawal came in July 1987. *Date 31st May 1985.*

Class 47/0 No 47207 on a down freight is pulling out of the extensive marshalling yards at Washwood Heath, which are situated to the north east of Birmingham. The M6 motorway viaduct dominates the background. No 47207 entered service at Crewe in August 1965 numbered D1857. It was named 'Bulmers of Hereford' in December 1987 and renamed 'The Felixstowe Partnership' in April 1998. From 1992 it was in and out of store several times before withdrawal came in April 2001. *Date 11th March 1987.*

There was a very heavy snowfall during the night of 9th February 1991, resulting in major disruption to rail services. This was the scene at Clay Cross five miles south of Chesterfield where the lines to Nottingham and Derby used to split. Today the junction has been moved about a mile to the north. A down freight hauled by Class 37/0 No 37048 had failed and Class 47/0 No 47053 had been sent to rescue it. No 47053 entered service in November 1964 as D1635, becoming 47053 in 1974. It carried two official names, 'Cory Brothers 1942-1992' in September 1992 and 'Dollands Moor International' in 1994. It was withdrawn in April 2001 and sold to Fragonset Railways, but was scrapped in 2007. *Date 9th February 1991.*

Class 25 No 25252 is at Peak Forest which used to be the summit of the old through Midland Main Line from Derby to Manchester Central. In the northbound direction it involved 19 miles of gradients around 1 in 100 with the last five miles at 1 in 90. Going south there were 18 miles of similar gradients from Cheadle Heath. Peak Forest has been the main centre for all the rail traffic coming out of the quarries in the Peak District since around 1860 and it is still very busy. There was a station which opened in 1867 and closed in March 1967. No 25252 is heading a small up freight and is seen from the road bridge which crosses the lines where the station once stood on the opposite side. Today the railway offices and crew facilities are situated here. No 25252 entered service numbered D7602 in February 1966 and had a short career which ended in March 1980. *Date 3rd July 1979.*

A fair amount of limestone dust is being blown across the countryside as this loaded train passes Chinley. It is descending the long steep gradient which over the years has resulted in some fatal and spectacular runaways. Chinley was once a busy station serving the main line to Derby and the one down the Hope Valley to Sheffield. It was originally opened on 1867 but resited in 1902. It is still open today, being served by a sparse local service from Manchester to Sheffield. Double headed class 40s on freight were rare but here Nos 40192 and 40126 are shown. No 40192 was new in May 1962, numbered D392 and allocated to Gateshead depot. It survived until 1985. No 40126 entered service as D326 in December 1960 at Crewe. It became a celebrity locomotive as it was the one involved in the 'Great Train Robbery' at Sears Green Crossing at Linslade on 8th August 1963. It was withdrawn in February 1984 and cut up by April, probably to avoid any chance of preservation. *Date 5th August 1983.*

The 15.00 Sheffield Midland–St Pancras is shown just south of Sheffield station beginning the five-mile climb at 1 in 100 to the summit at the south end of the one mile 266 yards long Bradway Tunnel. No 45137 entered service in November 1962 numbered D56 and was named 'The Bedfordshire and Hertfordshire Regiment (T.A.)' in December 1962. It remained in service until withdrawn in June 1987. It took seven years before it was finally scrapped. *Date 21st April 1979.*

About half way up the bank out of Sheffield Midland to Bradway Tunnel is a loop at Heeley where freight trains are frequently looped. On this day the Dewsbury to Earls sidings at Hope cement is stopped to let passenger trains pass. Ex-works Class 40 No 40040 is hauling the train. It was new in October 1959 to Gateshead depot and numbered D240. It spent all of its career allocated to the North Eastern Region until withdrawn in July 1980. *Date 27th May 1977.*

This train is the BOC Broughton Lane Sheffield to Ditton tanks which carried dangerous chemicals and was always double headed for safety reasons. It originally travelled by the Woodhead route before that closed and was then sent via the Hope Valley. This picture is taken from the signal box at New Mills South Junction, the train is taking the line to Marple and Romiley. Class 25/0 No 25298 is piloting class 40 No 40104. It entered service as D7648 in April 1966 and was withdrawn in March 1985. No 40104 had a slightly longer life, starting in December 1960 as D304 and ending in January 1985. *Date 29th April 1984.*

The Class 33s spent at least the first 20 years of their service almost exclusively working within the Southern Region. In the early 1980s their sphere of operation widened considerably. They were diagrammed to Portsmouth–Cardiff services from where they worked on to Swansea and beyond. They were also rostered on the North and West route to Crewe, plus the North Wales coast to Holyhead. No 33039, new as D6557, is entering Bangor station having just emerged from Belmont tunnel (648 yards long). Bangor station opened in 1848 and was once a busy railway centre serving several branch lines and having its own steam shed. Now it is just an intermediate station between Holyhead and Llandudno Junction. No 33039 went into service in June 1961 and was withdrawn in May 1989, ending up in Glasgow for scrapping. *Date 17th August 1985.*

The first station at Llandudno originally opened in 1858. A new station was built in 1882 which is still in use. It is at the end of a short branch which leaves the main line at Llandudno Junction and post-war became very busy, especially during the summer months. The level crossing at the Junction caused long delays to road traffic until it was eventually replaced by a flyover bridge. Class 31/4 No 31408 is approaching Llandudno and is crossing the well known Maesdu golf course, with the Conway hills in the background. No 31408 was new to Hornsey depot as D5646 in September 1960 and was cut up in March 2001. *Date 29th August 1989.*

The highlight of the day on the North Wales coast line on summer Saturdays in the late 1980s and early 1990s was the appearance of Class 20s on extra passenger workings. Here Nos 20160 and 20139 are leaving the west end of Rhyl station on the 08.15 Blyth Bridge to Llandudno. In the background can be seen the impressive Rhyl No 2 signal box with an up freightliner train from Holyhead passing. No 20139 was new in April 1966 as D8139 and 20160 in December 1966 as D8160; 20139 was withdrawn in May 1991 and sold to a French company CFD Industrie, Autun. It was eventually scrapped in the UK in 2010. No 20160 was withdrawn in December 1990. *Date 1st September 1989.*

The 10.05 from Manchester to Bangor is crossing the River Weaver on Frodsham viaduct (also called Weaver viaduct) before entering the 87 yards long tunnel and Frodsham station which opened in 1850. Class 40 No 40029 is in charge, which was new in August 1959 and numbered D229 and named 'Saxonia' in March 1963. It was withdrawn in April 1984. *Date 21st August 1982.*

Another view of Frodsham viaduct showing the River Weaver and a barge unloading. Class 47/3 No 47376 is heading east on a tank train which had probably come from Stanlow. No 47376 was one of the no-heat batch of class 47s, entering service in September 1965 numbered D1895. It can be seen to be carrying the unofficial name 'Skylark', but was officially named 'Freightliner 1995' in August 1995. Storage came in January 2000 and it eventually passed into preservation. *Date 28th June 1993.*

Tyseley set T404 in 1988 comprises a Class 115 vehicle, a Class 116 vehicle and a Class 127. It is running alongside the canal as it approachs Tipton, which is just over eight miles from Birmingham New Street on the Wolverhampton line. The station opened here in 1852. *Date 5th August 1990.*

Class 47/3 No 47318 has just passed through the 'Lever Brothers' factory complex before it passed under Warrington Bank Quay station on the WCML with a freight from the west. It will proceed into Latchford sidings a mile further on, where it will reverse before heading for the main sidings at Arpley. No 47318 was one of the batch of 81 class 47s built without heating. It entered service in January 1965 at Tinsley numbered D1799. Withdrawal came in July 1993 and it was scrapped in August 2004. *Date 22nd September 1987.*

Class 31/4 No 31405, is on the 15,45 departure to Sheffield via the Hope Valley. It is inside the splendid Manchester Piccadilly station which opened in May 1842 under the name Manchester Store Street. It was renamed Piccadilly in 1960, having previously been renamed London Road. No 31405 was based at Immingham depot at this time, along with others in the class for working the Cleethorpes–Manchester services via the Hope Valley line. New in April 1960 numbered D5606, it was named 'Mappa Mundi' in May 1991. It was one of the very few Class 31/4s to receive Intercity Main Line livery. It was withdrawn in April 1999 and cut up in April 2000. *Date 8th June 1984.*

Back in the 1970s the limestone trains out of Swinden Quarry at Rylstone, at the top end of what used to be the Grassington and Threshfield branch, were virtually entirely worked by double-headed Class 31/1s. The Quarry is just under seven miles from Skipton. Grassington and Threshfield station opened in July 1902. Passenger services were withdrawn in 1930, although Rambler specials were run until 1968. The line past Rylstone to Grassington closed in 1969. The branch is still very busy with limestone traffic. Class 37s took over from the Class 31s until the arrival of the Class 60s when double heading was no longer necessary. Today Class 66s are used. Class 31/0s Nos 31226 and 31109 are ready to leave with a train to Hull. No 31226 was new in September 1960 numbered D5652. It came to a spectacular end when in October 1988, coupled to No 31202, both ran away at Cricklewood sidings, went through the buffer stops down an embankment and into the London North Circular Road. No 31109 was allocated to Stratford at the time of this picture and entered service in April 1959 numbered D5527. *Date 30th April 1979.*

This is Capernwray Viaduct, which is two and a half miles out of Carnforth on the line to Wennington and Settle Junction. It carries the line over the River Keer. It currently only sees about half a dozen trains a day in each direction plus the empty stock movements from West Coast Railways and the occasional steam working. Freight traffic has long since been consigned to the history books, but back in 1981 there was this working from Barrow to the North East carrying chemicals which at one time used the Ilkley route from Skipton, but at this time was diagrammed via Leeds. Class 45/0 No 45004 was in charge on this day. It entered traffic in December 1960 numbered D77 and was named 'Royal Irish Fusilier' in September 1965. It was withdrawn in December 1985. *Date 12th December 1981.*

Due to engineering work on the WCML in 1989 south of Carnforth the vital steel traffic from Scotland was diverted over the Carnforth–Settle Junction line and then from Hellifield to Blackburn. This occurred over several weekends. The trains were worked by pairs of Class 20s, which were almost unknown on the route. I have heard it suggested that these were the most heavily loaded trains ever to work over the route. Nos 20028 and 20172 are at Clapham Common on the 5.25 Mossend to Dee Marsh. Both locomotives were allocated to Thornaby depot at the time, No 20172 carrying large numbers on the side. No 20028 spent eight years from new on the Scottish Region entering service in December 1959 as D8028. No 20172 arrived 7 years later in October 1966 as D 8172. It was withdrawn in October 1990 and cut up five years later. *Date 11th March 1989.*

The railways arrived at Grange-over-Sands, a fashionable Victorian resort, in 1857. It is situated on the line to Barrow in Furness about 10 miles from Carnforth. The days of through Barrow to London trains are now history, but here Class 47/4 No 47445 is leaving the station with an up service to Euston. It was new to the Eastern Region at Tinsley depot in March 1964 numbered D1561. It was withdrawn from Tinsley depot in July 1991, although it had been allocated to many other depots. *Date 5th May 1980.*

Diggle, on the Standedge TransPennine route is the setting for this picture of a Class 124 TransPennine DMU passing where there used to be an extensive goods yard. The station, which is just out of the picture to the right, opened in 1850 and closed in 1968. The canal tunnel started to the left of the train and the three other tunnels (mentioned on page 45) next to the station. Unfortunately none of these fine looking units which were built for the TransPennine services over this route in 1960 have passed into preservation. All the class had been withdrawn by the summer of 1984. *Date 15th April 1978.*

Class 45/1 No 45112 'The Royal Army Ordnance Corps', named in September 1965 is leaving the impressive Liverpool Lime Street station and is about to enter the equally impressive Lime Street cutting heading the 14.03 heading a TransPennine express. Class 31/4 No 31428 can be seen to the left. No 45112 was new in March 1962 as D61 and withdrawn in May 1987. It was eventually sold to the East Lancs Railway in 1991 and then sold on to Fragonset Railways in June 1999. *Date 14th June 1986.*

The West Coast Main line was frequently closed in Sundays between Wigan and Preston around this period. This resulted in trains being top and tailed between Wigan and Lostock Junction, where the trains would proceed to Preston via Chorley. The regular motive power for the dragging was Springs Branch Class 20s. Nos 20047 and 20210 have just arrived at the Junction where they will be detached. The 08.17 from Stoke to Blackpool will continue on its journey hauled in this case by Class 47/4 No 47537 'Sir Gwynedd/County of Gwynedd'. No 20047 was new to the Eastern Region in December 1959 numbered D8047. It was withdrawn in September 1991 and sold to RFS locomotives in France. It returned to the UK in August 1993 and eventually was overhauled and operated by DRS. No 20210 has a less interesting history. It entered traffic in April 1967 as D8310 and was withdrawn in April 1993. *Date 29th June 1986.*

During the 1980s and 1990s and into the early years of the new century, the West Coast main line was often closed north of Crewe at weekends. This resulted in the Liverpool and Scottish services and others being diverted by Stockport and Bolton. Ordsall Lane at Salford provided an excellent place to see all the diversions, with an impressive backdrop for photographs. Sadly the location is now covered by wires and masts after the electrification. The electric locomotives were dragged throughout the diversion. Here the down 'Royal Scot' with Class 87 No 87012 is being towed by Class 47/4 No 47477 and is about to take the chord round to Salford Crescent. No 47477 was new to the Western Region in July 1964 numbered D1607 and withdrawn in October 1992. *Date 8th September 1991.*

At the time of this photograph, engineering work north of Preston on the WCML resulted in services being diverted via the Settle and Carlisle, much to the delight of enthusiasts. This continued from the dieselisation of but in recent years buses were substituted along the M6 motorway. In the days when the new Class dominated the services in the late 1960s and up to 1974, when electrification was introduced on the WCML, they were frequently seen on the diverted trains. No D417 (later 50017) and before being named 'Royal Oak' is passing Settle Junction with the diverted down 'Royal Scot' at the start of the 'long drag' climb to Blea Moor. D417 built by English Electric arrived at Crewe April 1968. It was transferred to the Western Region in January 1976. Withdrawal came in July 1991 but it was reinstated for two months and withdrawn again. It was sold into preservation and worked the Northern Belle Pullman services on the network for a short period. *Date 29th November 1969.*

This Saturday on the Settle and Carlisle, when there were diversions, was one of the days when the weather produced all the seasons in one day, from a glorious sunny morning to rain and snow in the afternoon. Class 47/4 No 47540 has just passed Ais Gill summit (1169 feet) in a blizzard, with the 10.45 Euston–[...] Central. No 47540 carried several numbers and had an interesting end to its career. It was new in Ma[...] 1964 numbered D1723. Allocated No 47132 but not used and replaced to 47540 in 1974. It became 47[...] 1990 and reverted to 47540 in 1995. It received the name 'The Institution of Civil Engineers' in September 1991. It was first stored in October 1994, reinstated in April 1995 and moved to Brush Engineering for re-engining and conversion, but this never happened. After being moved around to several locations in stored status, it was considered withdrawn in 2002 and was sold in 2003, then stored in a yard by the A1 road where the Ripon–Northallerton railway once passed under the A1. The loco remained by the A1 for six years and then went on to the Wensleydale Railway between September 2009 and March 2016, when it was scrapped. *Date 2nd April 1983.*